# Ant to Zinnia
# Nature Activities

## Hyda Maria Dougherty

Tribal Eye Productions
Santa Ynez, CA

Ant to Zinnia Nature Activities

© 2014 Hyda Maria Dougherty

Printed in the USA

Tribal Eye Productions
P.O. Box 1123 / Santa Ynez, CA 93460
TribalEyePro@gmail.com


ISBN: 979-8-218-65123-7

# Acknowledgments

I am most grateful to my mother, Ms. Laura Dougherty (1903-1992) She taught and inspired thousands of children to learn how to read and write. Ms. Dougherty's dedication, compassion and creativity have been my motivation to offer these Nature's ABC books.

Many thanks to my grown children and hundreds of other children that I have taught and continue to teach as they help to keep me engaged, informed, and they are my best editors.

A special thanks to family: Larry, Marty and Kevin Parcell who have always been there when I needed them the most as have Manuel and Elizabeth Romero. I am also grateful to Marisela Romero for her interest and support of the ABC books both as a professional and as a parent.

My gratitude extends to Anna Marie Houser and to Phillip Haozous who have believed in me every step of the way and provided valuable feedback and innumerable resources.

My sincere appreciation to Gary Robinson, the publisher. Many thanks for the patience and guidance of the proofreaders: Michelle Martinez, Lauren Roberts and Shawn Newell.

I would like to recognize a few of the many friends that have contributed in so many ways: Tari Woods for a quiet, restorative place to stay for inspiration. Evelyn Jones who provides a serene place at her ranch for me to write and paint. Sylvia Chavez, an educator with valuable insights. Concha Allen, Patricia Sigala and Madi Sato influence my integration of music, art, and dance for children.

The Author

# ANT TO ZINNIA NATURE ACTIVITIES

This is an interactive handbook that goes with the *Ant to Zinnia Nature's ABC's* book. It has an easy to follow format. Children are able to learn at their own pace and the activities challenge them to move forward step by step. It is well suited for children ages 4-8 years old. It combines a number of teaching modalities based upon a sensory and tactile approach to learning that embraces nature and art while providing a solid foundation in reading and writing. It is especially well suited for early childhood education, special education and learning English as a second language.

The children are introduced first to letter recognition, the sounds of the letters and sound blending. They learn to write the letters, the words and draw a picture for each one. Children that have these basic skills can then move onto writing words, sentences and eventually create their own short stories. The purpose is to build their vocabulary and to improve their comprehension in a way that inspires them to explore and use their imaginations. They become critical thinkers by asking and answering questions.

The activities integrate art, music and movement. This helps to reinforce each lesson. One does not need to go out and purchase expensive art supplies for these activities. In fact since it is nature based it encourages a sustainable practice for our environment. Many of the materials can be collected right in your own homes and backyards. The use of recycled materials is encouraged. One is able to use what you have on hand to collect a treasure box of goodies. This box can include found objects such as: rocks, twigs, leaves, paper towel rolls, newspapers, magazines, ribbons, beads, etc.

A child may need guidance and help to read the instructions in each lesson but as their reading skills improve they will be able to provide themselves with hours of learning and entertainment. They eventually will be able to read the lessons and expand on them. This book is a guide, a support and a springboard to unlock even greater ideas to support a healthy and sustainable place for us all. Please feel free to include your favorite children's songs, dances and short stories both in a child's first language as well as in English.

I am grateful to my mother, Laura Dougherty who integrated music, stories and art into teaching children how to read and write with great success. She was an inspiration to many! I am thankful to all those who have supported the creation of this Literacy Arts Program.

*Hyda Maria Dougherty*

Lesson 1: **ANT**

**Objectives:**
Recognize the letter *a*. Introduce the short and long sounds of *a*.
Write the letter *a*. Write the word *ant*.
Draw an ant and learn about ants.
Write and recite words that begin with the letter *a*.
Build vocabulary and improve comprehension.

**Materials:**
Book of verses: Ant to Zinnia Nature's ABC's
ABC activity sheet for the letter *a*
Paper, crayons and egg cartons
Watercolor paints, brushes and markers
Scissors, pipe cleaners and pencil with sharp point

**Procedure:**
Read the verse for the word *ant* and show the illustration.
Pass out paper, crayons, and the activity sheet for the letter *a*.
Write the letter *a*. Write the word *ant*.
Draw an ant. Students do the same.
Write and recite, "*a* says *aa*" as in the words *ant, apple, after*.
This is the short sound of *a*.
The letter *a* also says its own name as in the words *ate, acorn, age*.
Write and say the sentence: *The ant ate an apple.*

**Activities:**
Where do ants live?
They live in underground ant colonies.
The queen ant has her own room.
The ants build under ground tunnels to connect the rooms.
Why is the queen ant important?
She lays the eggs for more ants to be born.
What do they eat?
They eat vegetation like grass, plants, and seeds.

Let's make an ant:
Cut a strip of 3 cups from a cardboard egg carton for the head and body of the ant.
Paint the cups red, black or any color. Let them dry.
Poke two holes on the top of the first cup using a sharp pencil. Push a short pipe cleaner one end into each hole from inside of the cup to make the antenna.
Use a sharp pencil to poke two holes across from each other on each of the 3 cups.
For the legs push a pipe cleaner through the holes of the first cup so that it extends out on each side. Do this for the other two cups. Draw eyes and mouth on with a marker.

# A a
ant

Lesson 2: **BAA**

**Objectives:**
Recognize the letter *b* and learn its sound.
Write the letter *b* and the word *baa*.
Draw a lamb and learn about sheep.
Write and recite words that begin with the letter *b*.
Practice sound blending and build vocabulary.

**Materials:**
Book of verses: Ant to Zinnia Nature's ABC's
ABC activity sheet for the letter *b*
Paper, crayons, scissors
Recycled cardboard, glue, different colors of yarn (scraps are fine)

**Procedure:**
Read the verse for the word *baa* and show the illustration.
Pass out paper, crayons, and the activity sheet for the letter *b*.
Write the letter *b* and the word *baa*.
Draw a lamb. Students do the same.
Write and recite, "*b* says *buh*" as in the words *bug*, *butterfly*, and *bus*.

**Activities:**
One sheep is called a lamb.
Where do they live?
They live in the mountains, farms and meadows.
What do they say?
Baa! Baa!
What do they eat?
They eat grass.
What do we use their fleece for?
The fleece is spun into wool. We use the yarn to make clothes and blankets.

Let's make a picture with yarn:
Draw a flower, sheep, or design on cardboard.
Cut different colors and sizes of yarn.
Put a small amount of glue on a section of the design and lay yarn on the glue.
Continue to do this until your design is filled in with different colors of yarn.

# B b

baa

Lesson 3: **CAT**

**Objectives:**
Recognize the letter *c* and learn its sound.
Write the letter *c* and the word *cat*.
Draw a cat and learn about different types of cats.
Practice sound blending and build vocabulary.

**Materials:**
Book of verses: Ant to Zinnia Nature's ABC's
ABC activity sheet for the letter *c*
Paper and crayons
Pictures of different kinds of cats

**Procedure:**
Read the verse for the word *cat* and show the illustration.
Pass out paper, crayons and activity sheet for the letter *c*.
Write the letter *c* and the word *cat*.
Draw a cat. Students do the same.
Write and recite, "*c* says *cuh*" as in the words *cap*, *cab*, and *can*.
Write and use each word in a sentence.

**Activities:**
What is the difference between domestic cats and wild cats?
Domestic cats are pets. Wild cats live in their natural habitats.
How do cats communicate?
They meow, growl or hiss. They put their tails up and swish them back and forth.
How do they protect themselves?
They run, jump and climb walls or trees to get away from other animals.
Their sharp claws and teeth are also used to protect themselves.
How do they show affection?
They purr, lick, or give gentle love bites.

Let's be like a cat:
Creep on your belly and then roll onto your back.
Sit very still. Pretend you are watching a lizard and then pounce as if to catch it.
Meow, growl and hiss like a cat.
Stretch your arms up overhead like you are reaching and looking up a tree at a bird.
Draw your favorite kind of cat: lion, tiger, bobcat or domestic cat.

# C c

## cat

Lesson 4: **DUCK**

**Objectives:**
    Recognize the letter *d* and learn its sound.
    Write the letter *d* and the word *duck.*
    Draw a duck and learn about its habitat.
    Practice sound blending and improve comprehension.

**Materials:**
    Book of verses: Ant to Zinnia Nature's ABC's
    ABC activity sheet of letter *d*
    Paper and crayons
    Recycled plastic bags or paper bags and gloves

**Procedure:**
    Read the verse for the word *duck* and show the illustration.
    Pass out paper, crayons, and the activity sheet for the letter *d.*
    Write the letter *d* and the word *duck.* Sound it out. Students do the same.
    Write and recite, "*d* says *duh*" as in the words *dad, dog,* and *dig.*
    Write and use each word in a sentence.

**Activities:**
    Visit a pond or lake. Discuss safety around water.
    Walk quietly so as not to disturb the wild life.
    Stay a few feet away from the edge of the water.
    Where do ducks live?
    They live on lakes, ponds, rivers and seas.
    Where do they lay their eggs?
    They lay their eggs in the grass.
    What do they eat?
    They eat seeds, leaves, insects, and fish eggs.
    How do they get around from place to place?
    Ducks have webbed feet. This allows them to paddle and swim.
    They can fly for miles and miles to get to warmer climates in winter.

    Let's clean up:
    Take a walk and use recycled bags and gloves to pick up litter.
    Recycle plastic bottles, tin cans, and paper.
    Discuss why it is important not to litter.

# D d
## duck

LESSON 5: **EGG**

**Objectives:**
    Recognize the letter *e*. Introduce the short and long sounds of *e*.
    Write the letter *e* and the word *egg*.
    Draw an egg and discuss what animals lay eggs.
    Build vocabulary and improve comprehension.

**Materials:**
    Book of verses: Ant to Zinnia Nature's ABC's
    ABC activity sheet for the letter *e*
    Paper, crayons, glue, scissors
    Lids of egg cartons or lightweight cardboard
    A sample of collected feathers, pebbles, leaves and beads

**Procedure:**
    Read the verse for the word *egg* and show the illustration.
    Pass out paper, crayons, and the activity sheet for the letter *e*.
    Write the letter *e* and the word *egg*.
    Draw an egg.  Students do the same.
    Write and recite, "*e* says *eh*" as in the words *egg*, *exit*, and *elephant*.
    This is the short sound of *e*.
    The letter *e* also says its own name as in the words *eagle, eat, eleven*.
    Students may copy and/or color the activity sheet for the letter *e*.

**Activities:**
    What animals lay eggs?
    Reptiles like snakes and lizards.
    All birds lay eggs and some fish lay eggs.
    There are different colors and sizes of eggs.
    How do some people like to cook eggs?
    They can be hard-boiled, fried, scrambled or made into omelets.

    Let's make eggs and decorate them with natural objects:
    Cut a few different size egg shapes out of the cardboard or egg carton.
    Color the cardboard eggs.
    Collect leaves, grass, pebbles and found objects in nature.
    Glue these onto your colored cardboard eggs.

E e

egg

Lesson 6: **FROG**

**Objectives:**
Recognize the letter *f* and learn its sound.
Write the letter *f* and the word *frog*.
Draw a frog and learn about frogs.
Write and recite words that begin with the letter *f*.
Practice sound blending and build vocabulary.

**Materials:**
Book of verses: Ant to Zinnia Nature's ABC's
ABC activity sheet for the letter *f*
Paper, crayons, watercolors
Paintbrushes and containers for water

**Procedure:**
Read the verse for the word *frog* and show the illustration.
Pass out paper, crayons, and the activity sheet for the letter *f*.
Write the letter *f* and the word *frog*.
Draw a frog. Students do the same.
Write and recite, "*f* says *fuh*" as in the words *frog*, *fish*, and *fan*.
Write and use each word in a sentence.
Students may copy and/or color the activity sheet for the letter *f*.

**Activities:**
Where do frogs live?
They live in ponds, lakes, and rivers.
What do they eat?
They like to eat insects.
What are the babies called?
They are called tadpoles.
What other animals live in and around a pond?
There are fish, birds and insects.

Let's visit a pond:
Take a field trip to a nearby pond. Sit quietly and listen to all the sounds.
What do you hear? What do you see?
It is said that frogs call in the rain. Sing ribbit, ribbit, grr-ump, grr-ump!
Color or paint a picture of a pond with frogs, fish, grass and insects.

F f
Frog

Lesson 7: **GO** green

**Objectives:**
Recognize the letter *g* and learn its sound.
Write the letter *g* and the word *go*.
Draw a plant for the words *go green*.
Write and recite words that begin with the letter *g*.
Learn about a variety of plants.

**Materials:**
Book of verses: Ant to Zinnia Nature's ABC's
ABC activity sheet for the letter *g*
Sketchpads, colored pencils or crayons
Pinecone and a pot to plant a tree
Dirt and or potting soil and water

**Procedure:**
Read the verse for the word *go* and show the illustration.
Pass out paper, crayons, and the activity sheet for the letter *g*.
Write the letter *g* and the word *go*.
Draw green trees with grass. Students do the same.
Write and recite, "*g* says *guh*" as in the words *go*, *goat*, and *gal*.
Write and use each word in a sentence.

**Activities:**
Why are trees important?
Trees provide oxygen for us to breathe.
They also provide shelter and shade for many animals.
What are some different kinds of trees?
There are pine, fruit, aspen, maple and oak trees.
Go for a walk and sketch different trees. Identify them by name.

Let's grow a tree:
Pinecones that have dropped to the ground can be found in your neighborhood, in the parks or when accompanied by an adult in the woods or mountains. You only need one.
Fill a pot almost full with dirt/potting soil.
Plant the cone in the pot so most of it stands out and only a little is in the dirt.
Give it a little water everyday but not too much or the cone will rot.
Place it near a window where it can get some sun. Soon a tiny tree will grow!

# G g

go green

Lesson 8: **HEN**

**Objectives:**
Recognize the letter *h* and learn its sound.
Write the letter *h* and the word *hen*.
Draw a hen and learn about hens.
Write and recite words that begin with the letter *h*.

**Materials:**
Book of verses: Ant to Zinnia Nature's ABC's
ABC activity sheet for the letter *h*
White paper or newsprint, crayons
Paintbrushes and watercolor paint

**Procedure:**
Read the verse for the word *hen* and show the illustration.
Pass out paper, crayons, and the activity sheet for the letter *h*.
Write the letter *h* and the word *hen*.
Draw a hen. Students do the same.
Write and recite, "*h* says *huh*" as in the words *hat, hen,* and *hop*.
Use these words in a sentence: *Have you ever seen a hen wear a hat and go hop, hop?*

**Activities:**
Where do hens live?
They live on farms in a hen house or chicken coop.
What are the males, females and babies called?
The males are called roosters and the females are called hens.
The babies are called chicks.
What do they eat?
They eat insects, grain, corn, and seeds.
What is a broody hen?
A hen that sits fast on her eggs day and night, leaving only once a day to eat and drink.
How long can you sit quietly in one spot?

Let's make a hen out of your handprint with watercolor paint:
Put paint in the palm of your hand.
Use a paintbrush to spread the paint over the palm of your hand and fingers.
Press your painted hand on a white sheet of paper.
Use your fingers or the brush to fill in any empty places not covered with paint.
The thumbprint is the head of your hen. Add a comb, beak and eyes to your hen.
Have fun and make more than one hen.

# Hh
## hen

Lesson 9: **IGLOO**

**Objectives**:
Recognize the letter *i* .
Introduce the short and long sounds of *i*.
Write the letter *i* and the word *igloo*.
Learn about the Inuit Indians.
Write and recite words that have the short sound of *i*.
Build vocabulary and improve comprehension.

**Materials:**
Book of verses: Ant to Zinnia Nature's ABC's
ABC activity sheet for the letter *i*
Pencils, glue and cotton balls
Lightweight cardboard

**Procedure:**
Read the verse for the word *igloo* and show the illustration.
Pass out paper, crayons, and the activity sheet for the letter *i*.
Write the letter *i* and the word *igloo*.
Draw an igloo.  Students do the same.
Write and recite, "*i* says *ih*" as in the words *Indian, Inuit*, and *igloo*.
This is the short sound of *i*.
The letter *i* also says its own name as in the words *ice, icicle, and idea*.
Use these words in a sentence: *Inuit Indians live in igloos made of ice blocks.*

**Activities:**
The Inuit Indians live in modern-day homes as well as igloos made of ice.
Look at a map or globe and find Alaska.
Inuit Indians hunt caribou and fish for food.
They build igloos out of ice blocks.
Some use sleds pulled by dogs to get around.
*Igloo* is the Inuit Indian word for *home*.

Let's make igloos:
Draw or trace an igloo like the one in the activity sheet.
Glue cotton balls on the igloo drawing and leave an opening for the door.
Complete your picture by painting or coloring the ocean and fish near the igloo.

# I i

igloo

Lesson 10: **JAY**

**Objectives:**
>Recognize the letter *j* and learn its sound.
>Write the letter *j* and the word *jay*.
>Learn words that begin with the letter *j*.
>Use these words in a sentence.
>Draw and learn about jays.

**Materials:**
>Book of verses: Ant to Zinnia Nature's ABC's
>ABC activity sheet for the letter *j*
>Crayons or watercolor paint and paintbrushes
>Toilet paper rolls and small pebbles
>Construction paper or lightweight cardboard

**Procedure:**
>Read the verse for the word *jay* and show the illustration.
>Pass out paper, crayons, and the activity sheet for the letter *j*.
>Write the letter *j* and the word *jay*.
>Draw the jay. Students do the same.
>Write and recite, "*j* says *juh*" as in the words *jump*, *jog*, and *jig*.
>Use these words in a sentence: *Jenny likes to jump rope, dance a jig and jog.*

**Activities:**
>What are some different kinds of jays?
>Mexican jays, steller jays, brown jays, green jays, and blue jays
>What do jays eat?
>They like nuts, sunflower seeds, cherries, wild grapes, and small berries.
>What do blue jays say?
>They have a "whisper song", a soft medley of clicks, chucks, whines, and more.

>Let's make shakers:
>Color or paint a t-paper roll.
>Draw and cut out cardboard circles to fit each end of the rolls. And paint them.
>Glue a circle to one end of the t-paper roll and fill it with about ¼ small pebbles.
>Seal the roll by gluing the other cardboard circle to the open end.

>Shake your rattle gently back and forth as you sing this song:
>Pretty little blue jay where do you go?
>I go said the blue jay, as she flew on high to see if my color matches the sky!

J j

jay

Lesson 11: **KITE**

**Objectives:**

Recognize the letter *k* and learn its sound.
Write the letter *k* and the word *kite*.
Draw and make a kite, and if weather permits, fly it.
Write sentences with words that begin with *k*.

**Materials**:

Book of verses: Ant to Zinnia Nature's ABC's
ABC activity sheet for the letter *k*
Two sticks per student and masking tape
Newspaper, roll of string and ribbons

**Procedure:**

Read the verse for the word *kite*, and show the illustration.
Write the letter *k* and the word *kite*.
Draw a kite. Students do the same.
Write and recite, "*k* says *kuh*" as in the words *kid*, *kite*, and *kangaroo*.
Write and use each word in a sentence: *A kite is a bird in the hawk family.*
Students may copy and/or color the activity sheet for the letter *k*.

**Activities:**

What makes a kite stay up in the air?  The wind catches the kite so it goes up and down and it can sail in the sky. You cannot see or hold the wind but you can feel it. Birds need the wind to be able to fly and glide across the sky. Plants need the wind to scatter their seeds. We need the wind to cool things down on a hot day. The wind blows in the clouds so we will have rain.

Let's make a kite:
Place two sticks on a flat surface. The horizontal stick is shorter.
They will look like the lower case "t". Tape the sticks together.
An adult draws cuts out a diamond shaped pattern.
Trace the diamond shape pattern onto newspaper and cut it out.
Lay the diamond shape newspaper on a flat surface and tape the sticks to it.
Glue ribbons or strip of papers to the end of the kite for the kite tail.
Tie the roll of string onto the sticks where they cross together to form a "t".
Enjoy flying your kite on a windy day.

# K k
## kite

Lesson 12: **LOLLIPOP**

**Objectives:**
Recognize the letter *l* and learn its sound.
Write the letter *l* and the word *lollipop*.
Draw lollipops of different shapes and colors.
Write and recite words that begin with the letter *l*.
Learn about fruit flavors of lollipops.

**Materials:**
Book of verses: Ant to Zinnia Nature's ABC's
ABC activity sheet for the letter *l*
Paper, crayons or watercolors
Pictures of fruits: lemons, apples, oranges, etc.

**Procedure:**
Read the verse for the word *lollipop* and show the illustration.
Pass out paper, crayons, and the ABC activity sheet for the letter *l*.
Write the letter *l* and the word *lollipop*.
Draw a lollipop. Students do the same.
Write and recite, "*l* says *luh*" as in the words *lollipop*, *log*, and *love*.
Write and use each word in a sentence: *We like lollipops.*

**Activities:**
Lollipops have fruit flavors like cherry, grape, and apple.
Where does fruit grow?
Fruit grows on trees, vines and bushes.
What kind of fruit grows on trees?
Apples, oranges, peaches, plums, limes and lemons grow on trees.
What fruit grows on vines?
Grapes, different kinds of berries and melons grow on vines.
What else besides lollipops are made with fruit?
Jelly, popsicles, and smoothies are made out of fruit.

Let's have fun with lollipops:
Color or paint lollipops shaped like different kinds of fruits such as: oranges, apples, grapes, lemons, limes, watermelons or whatever your favorite kind of fruit is.

# Ll

lollipop

Lesson 13: **MONKEY**

**Objectives:**

Recognize the letter *m* and learn its sound.
Write the letter *m* and the word *monkey*.
Draw a monkey and learn about monkeys.
Write and recite words that begin with the letter *m*.
Use words that begin with *m* in sentences.

**Materials:**

Book of verses: Ant to Zinnia Nature's ABC's
ABC activity sheet for the letter *m*
Dry-erase board or chalkboard
Paper and crayons
Pictures and photos of monkeys in their natural habitats

**Procedure:**

Read the verse for the word *monkey* and show the illustration.
Pass out paper, crayons, and the activity sheet for the letter *m*.
Write the letter *m* and the word *monkey*.
Draw a monkey. Students do the same.
Write and recite, "*m* says *mm*" as in the words *man*, *mat*, and *mask*.
Write and use these words in sentences: *The man sat on a mat.*

**Activities:**

Where do monkeys live?
They live in the jungle and in the forest.
What do they eat?
They eat fruit, leaves, and nuts.
How are they like us?
They take care of each other and live in families.

Let's play Monkey See, Monkey Do:
One person is the lead monkey and pretends to act and sound like a monkey.
Monkeys grunt and make squeaking sounds to express happiness, excitement and
other emotions like we do. The other children imitate what the lead monkey does.
Let everyone take a turn being the lead monkey. They can move and sound like a
variety of different animals. It is fun to guess what animal is being imitated.

# M m

# monKey

Lesson14: **NEST**

**Objectives:**
    Recognize the letter *n* and learn its sound.
    Write the letter *n* and the word *nest*.
    Learn words that begin with the letter *n*.
    Collect materials to build a nest.

**Materials:**
    Book of verses: Ant to Zinnia Nature's ABC's
    ABC activity sheet for the letter *n*
    Paper and crayons
    A sample of collected items in nature: twigs, grass and small feathers

**Procedure:**
    Read the verse for the word *nest* and show the illustration.
    Pass out paper, crayons, and the activity sheet for *n*.
    Write the letter *n* and the word *nest*.
    Draw a nest. Students do the same.
    Write and recite, "*n* says *nn*" as in the words *nine*, *number*, and *nest*.
    Write and use each word in a sentence.

**Activities:**
    What are some different types of houses that people live in?
    People live in apartments, houses, trailers, adobe homes, hogans and yurts.
    What materials are used to build homes?
    Many kinds of material are used to make homes such as: wood, mud, straw, metal, glass, brick, concrete and glass.
    What are different homes that animals live in?
    Their homes are in caves, grass, trees, underground, and even in water.

    Let's go on a nature treasure hunt to build a bird's nest:
    Collect soft flexible straw, twigs, long grass, vines, cotton and small feathers.
    Bend straw, long grass and vines into a circle like shape.
    Use string to hold the shape of the nest together. Add small feathers and cotton.
    Use organic materials in nature to build your nest.
    Place your nest in a tree as high off the ground as you can. Please do not touch or disturb any nests you find in nature.

# N n
## nest

Lesson 15: **OCTOPUS**

**Objectives:**
    Recognize the letter *o*. Introduce the short and long sounds of *o*.
    Write the letter *o* and the word *octopus*.
    Learn words that begin with the letter *o*.
    Use words that begin with *o* in sentences.
    Draw an octopus and learn about the octopus.
    Paint an ocean scene with octopi of different colors.

**Materials:**
    Book of verses: Ant to Zinnia Nature's ABC's
    ABC activity sheet for the letter *o*
    Paper and crayons
    Large sheet of paper for painting
    Watercolors, paintbrushes, and containers for water

**Procedure:**
    Read the verse for the word *octopus* and show the illustration.
    Pass out the activity sheet for the letter *o*.
    Write the letter *o* and the word *octopus*. Draw an octopus.
    Write and recite, "*o* says *ah*" as in the words *off, otter and octopus*.
    The letter *o* also says its own name as in the words *open, orange, and ocean*.
    Write and use these words in sentences: *An otter and an octopus live in the ocean.*

**Activities:**
    What is more than one octopus called?
    They are called octopi.
    Where do octopus live?
    They live in oceans and in the deep blue sea.
    What do they eat?
    They eat crab, lobster and shrimp.
    How does an octopus catch its food?
    The octopus has eight tentacles that are like long arms.
    The tentacles have suction cups so that they can hold on to their food.
    How do they protect themselves from predators?
    They change colors so they blend in with their surroundings and are hard to see.
    An octopus can release a big cloud of black ink and hide inside it.

    Let's paint octopi:
    Paint colorful octopi and fish in the ocean include shells and seaweed in your picture.

# O o

## octopus

Lesson 16: **PIG**

**Objectives:**

Recognize the letter *p* and learn its sound.
Write the letter *p* and the word *pig*.
Write and recite words that begin with the letter *p*.
Draw a pig and learn about pigs.
Build vocabulary and improve comprehension.

**Materials:**

Book of verses: Ant to Zinnia Nature's ABC's
ABC activity sheet for the letter *p*
Paper, crayons, and small paper bags
Pink watercolor paint, paintbrush and water
Pink construction paper and black markers

**Procedure:**

Read the verse for the word *pig* and show the illustration.
Pass out paper, crayons, and the activity sheet for the letter *p*.
Write the letter *p* and the word *pig*.
Draw a pig. Students do the same.
Write and recite, "*p* says *puh*" as in the words *pig*, *pat*, and *pot*.
Write and use each word in a sentence.

**Activities:**

What do pigs eat?
Pigs eat plants and small rodents like mice and squirrels.
What are the males, females and babies called?
The males are boars. The females are sows. The babies are piglets.
How do they clean themselves?
They roll in the mud to clean themselves.
How do pigs sleep?
They snuggle close to one another to sleep and to stay warm.

Let's make a pig:
Paint or color a paper bag pink, grey, yellow or multi colors.
Cut out small pink ears and a round nose out of pink construction paper.
Glue the nose and ears onto the paper bag. Use black marker for the eyes.
Cut little feet out of pink construction paper and glue onto the bottom of the paper bag.

P p

pig

Lesson 17: **QUAIL**

**Objectives:**
Recognize the letter *q* and learn its sound.
Write the letter *q* and the word *quail*.
Draw a quail and learn about feathers.
Build vocabulary and improve comprehension.

**Materials:**
Book of verses: Ant to Zinnia Nature's ABC'
ABC activity sheet for the letter *q*
Paper, crayons, watercolor paint
Variety of colored construction and tissue papers
Glue, scissors and recycled paper or lightweight cardboard

**Procedure:**
Read the verse for the word *quail* and show the illustration.
Pass out paper, crayons, and the activity sheet for the letter *q*.
Write the letter *q* and the word *quail*.
Draw a quail. Students do the same.
Write and recite, "*q* says *quh*" as in the words *quail*, *quack* and *quick*.
Write and use each word in a sentence: *Quail feathers are used to make quill pens.*

**Activities:**
Where do quails live?
They live in wild grasses, bushes, woodlands and forests.
What do quails eat?
They mostly eat seeds, berries, fruits and insects.
Where are good places to find any kind of bird feathers?
Feathers can be found in your backyard, on walks in nature and near rivers or ponds.
What is a quill?
A quill is any of the main wing or tail feathers of a bird.

Let's make feathers:
Draw a feather.
Using a variety of colored papers draw and cut out feathers of different sizes.
Glue your feathers onto recycled paper to make a collage.
You may add feathers to your collage that you find on your walks.
Only collect feathers that are not from endangered species like eagles.

# Q q
## quail

Lesson 18: **RABBIT**

**Objectives:**
Recognize the letter *r* and learn its sound.
Write the letter *r* and the word *rabbit*.
Draw a rabbit and learn about rabbits.
Write and recite words that begin with the letter *r*.
Use these words in sentences.

**Materials:**
Book of verses: Ant to Zinnia Nature's ABC's
ABC activity sheet for the letter *r*
Crayons and paper
Carrots, shallow dishes, and pebbles

**Procedure:**
Read the verse for the word *rabbit* and show the illustration.
Pass out paper, crayons, and the activity sheet for the letter *r*.
Draw the rabbit like the one in the activity sheet. Students do the same.
Write and recite, "*r* says *rr*" as in the words *rabbit*, *run*, and *red*.
Write and use these words in sentences.

**Activities:**
What are male, female and baby rabbits called?
A male rabbit is a buck.  A female rabbit is a doe.
A baby rabbit is called a kit or a kitten.
Where do they live?
They live underground in burrows.
How many babies do rabbits have at one time?
Rabbits can have 20-40 babies at one time.
How many different kinds of rabbits are there?
There are 45 different kinds of breeds of rabbits.
What do rabbits like to eat?
They eat weeds, grass, clover, wildflowers and vegetables.
They also like to eat the green tops of carrots.

Let's grow plants from carrot tops:
An adult cuts the top off of several carrots. Place pebbles in a shallow dish. Cover the pebbles with a little water and add the carrot tops. The pebbles will hold them in place. Make sure they always have a little water in the dish and sunlight. The green carrot tails will start to grow in one week.

# R r
# rabbit

Lesson 19: **SNAKE**

**Objectives**:

Recognize the letter *s* and learn its sound.
Write the letter *s* and the word *snake*.
Write and recite words that begin with the letter *s*.
Use these words in sentences to improve comprehension.
Draw a picture of a snake.
Learn about snakes.

**Materials:**

Book of verses: Ant to Zinnia Nature's ABC's
ABC activity sheet for the letter *s*
Paper, crayons, newspapers
Clay, play dough, or modeling clay

**Procedure:**

Read the verse for the word *snake* and show the illustration.
Pass out paper, crayons, and the activity sheet for the letter *s*.
Write the letter *s* and the word *snake*.
Draw a snake. Students do the same.
Write and recite, "*s* says *ss*" as in the words *snake*, *skunk*, and *swan*.
Write and use each word in a sentence: *The snake says, "Sss."*

**Activities:**

What do snakes eat?
They eat mice, birds and frogs.
Some snakes use poisonous venom to kill their prey.
Snakes have poor eyesight and smell with their tongue.
Where do snakes live?
They live in forests, deserts and in bodies of waters.
Why do snakes have different patterns and colors?
This makes them almost invisible to predators.

Let's make a snake:
An adult covers a table, floor, or work area with newspapers for easy cleanup.
You get a handful of clay. You can roll the clay into a ball.
The ball of clay is pressed with the palm of the hand and rolled back and forth.
This creates a long rope like the shape of a snake.
You can make other animals and shapes with the clay.

S s

snake

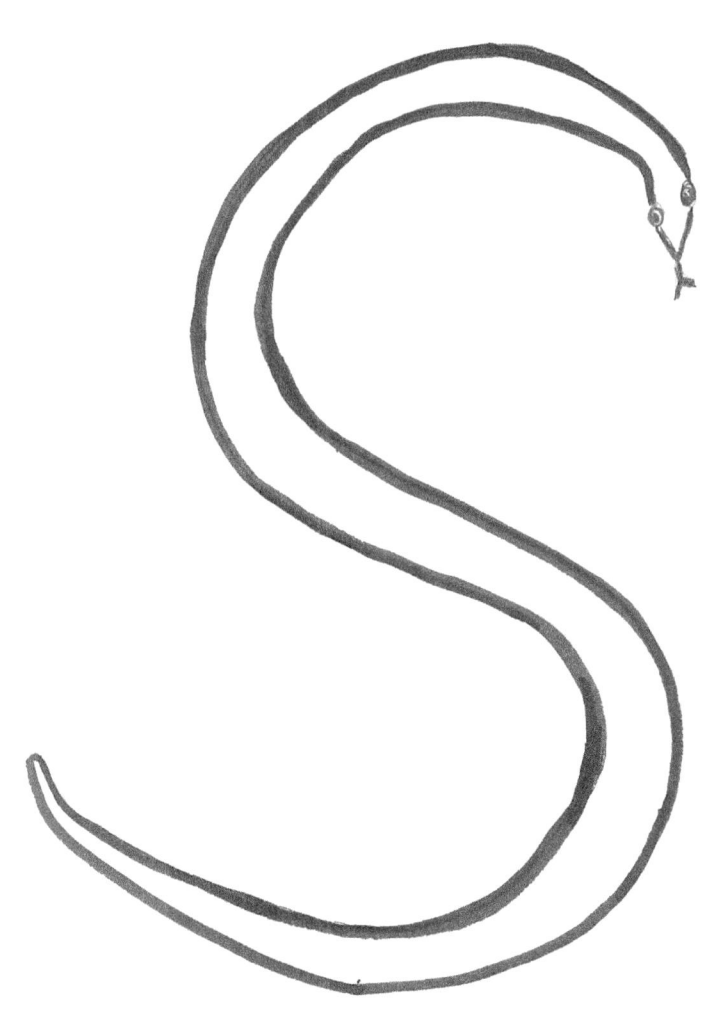

Lesson 20: **TURTLE**

**Objectives:**
Recognize the letter *t* and learn its sound.
Write the letter *t* and the word *turtle*.
Draw a turtle and learn about turtles.
Write and recite words that begin with the letter *t*.
Use these words in sentences to improve comprehension.

**Materials:**
Book of verses: Ant to Zinnia Nature's ABC's
ABC activity sheet for the letter *t*
Crayons, paper, and scissors
Construction paper or light cardboard-like poster board
Popsicle sticks and glue

**Procedure:**
Read the verse for the word *turtle* and show the illustration.
Pass out paper, crayons, and the activity sheet for the letter *t*.
Write the letter *t* and the word *turtle*.
Draw a turtle. Students do the same.
Write and recite, "*t* says *tuh*" as in the words *tag*, *tug*, and *tap*.
Write and use each word in a sentence: *We like to play tag.*

**Activities:**
Where do turtles live?
They live in the desert; turtles also live in the sea or in fresh water.
Why do turtles have hard shells?
Turtles have hard shells for protection.
They pull their heads, tails, and legs inside their shells when in danger.
What do turtles eat?
Some turtles only eat plants. Some eat insects, fish or frogs.

Let's make a turtle puppet:
Draw or trace the turtle in the activity sheet or draw your own.
Color the turtle and cut it out.
Glue a stick to the back of the turtle and use it as a puppet.
Make other puppet animals and have a puppet show.

# Tt

## turtle

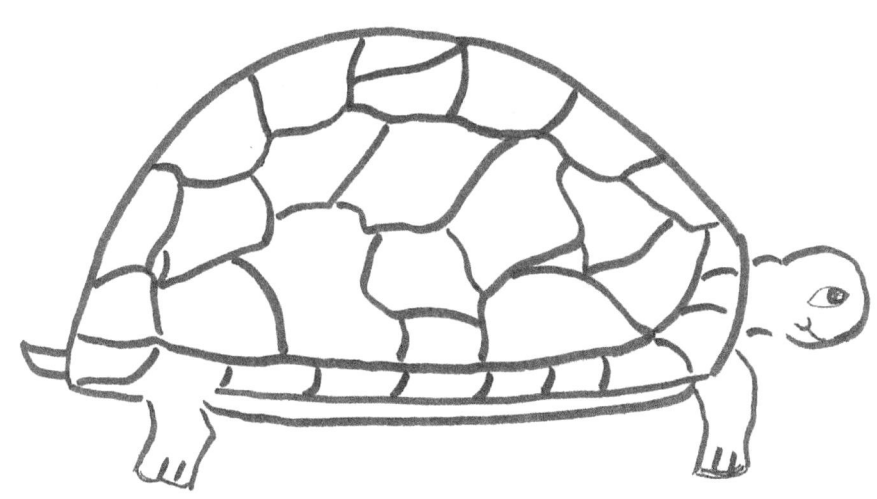

Lesson 21: **UMBRELLA**

**OBJECTIVES:**

Recognize the letter *u* and learn its sound.
Write the letter *u* and the word *umbrella*.
Draw an umbrella and discuss different kinds of weather.
Write and recite words that begin with the letter *u*.
Learn words that have the long and short sound of *u*.
Use these words in sentences to improve comprehension.

**Materials:**

Book of verses: Ant to Zinnia Nature's ABC's
ABC activity sheet for the letter *u*
Paper and crayons

**Procedure:**

Read the verse for the word *umbrella* and show the illustration.
Pass out paper, crayons, and the activity sheet for the letter *u*.
Write the letter *u* and the word *umbrella*.
Draw an umbrella. Students do the same.
Write and recite, "*u* says *uh*" as in the words *up*, *under*, and *umpire*.
The letter *u* *also* says its own name as in the words *use, universe, unicorn*.
Use the long and short sound of these words in sentences.

**Activities:**

What are umbrellas used for?
They are used to protect us from getting soaked in the rain.
They also protect us from the sun.
What are some different kinds of weather patterns?
The weather changes from season to season:
It is warm and rainy in the spring. It is hot in the summer.
It is cooler in the fall and it is cold and snowy in the winter.

Let's draw:
Draw an umbrella.
Draw big raindrops.
Draw the sun shining.
It can be raining and the sun shining!

# U u

## umbrella

Lesson 22: **VASE**

**Objectives:**
    Recognize the letter *v* and learn its sound.
    Write the letter *v* and the word *vase*.
    Learn to make tissue paper flowers.
    Make a vase for the flowers.
    Write and recite words that begin with the letter *v*.
    Use these words in sentences.

**Materials:**
    Book of verses: Ant to Zinnia Nature's ABC's
    ABC activity sheet for the letter *v*
    Paper and crayons
    Plastic water bottles for vases
    Yarn, beads, shells and/or sequins and glue to decorate recycled plastic bottles
    Different colors of tissue paper
    Green pipe cleaners

**Procedure:**
    Read the verse for the word vase and show the illustration.
    Pass out paper, crayons, and the activity sheet for the letter *v*.
    Write the letter *v* and the word *vase*.
    Draw a vase. Students do the same.
    Write and recite, "*v* says *vuh*" as in the words *violet, van,* and *violin.*
    Write and use each word in a sentence.

**Activities:**
    Let's make tissue paper flowers and a vase:
    Paint and decorate plastic bottles with yarn, beads, shells and or sequins.
    Set it aside and let it dry.  Now make tissue paper flowers.
    An adult cuts different colors of tissue papers into 6"x 6" squares for you.
    Stack 6–8 tissue paper squares of different colors together.
    Fold the tissue papers back and forth like a fan.
    Tie a pipe cleaner around the middle of the stack of tissue papers.
    Gently separate each tissue paper to form a flower.
    The flowers can then be put into the vase that you have made.

# Vv
## vase

Lesson 23: **WHALE**

**Objectives:**
 Recognize the letter *w* and learn its sound.
 Write the letter *w* and the word *whale*.
 Write and recite words that begin with the letter *w*.
 Use these words in sentences to build vocabulary.

**Materials:**
 Book of verses: Ant to Zinnia Nature's ABC's
 ABC activity sheet for letter *w*
 Paper and crayons
 Scissors and glue
 Optional: sand, pebbles and small seashells
 Construction paper: blue, brown, green and various colors

**Procedure:**
 Read the verse for the word *whale* and show the illustration.
 Pass out paper, crayons and the activity sheet for the letter *w*.
 Write the letter *w* and the word *whale*.
 Draw a whale. Students do the same.
 Write and recite, "*w* says *wuh*" as in the words *water*, *wind*, and *whisper*.
 Write and use each word in a sentence.

**Activities:**
 Whales are the largest mammals in the world.
 They can grow to 90 feet and weigh as much as 24 elephants!
 Some whales can live for 100-200 years.
 Can you sing the blue whale's song: woom, woom, oop oop, moo?
 What is one of the biggest threats to the health and well being of ocean life?
 Plastic is one of the biggest threats to all fish.
 Plastic is poisonous for fish to eat. They can get tangled in the plastic.
 We can make a difference by cutting our usage of plastic and recycling all plastic.
 Efforts are being made to clean up the tons of plastic now in our oceans and seas.

 Let's make an ocean scene:
 A sheet of blue construction paper will serve as the ocean.
 Cut out sand from brown construction paper and glue to the bottom of blue paper.
 Cut out seaweed out of green construction paper and glue to the background.
 Draw and cut out a whale out of light blue paper. The activity sheet whale can be used as a pattern. Glue the whale on the blue paper. Draw and cut out colorful fish from construction paper such as starfish, clown fish, and angelfish. Glue these in your ocean scene.

# W w
# whale

Lesson 24: **X-RAY**

**Objectives:**
>   Recognize the letter *x* and learn its sound.
>   Write the letter *x* and the word *x-ray*.
>   Draw an x-ray fish and make a banner.
>   Write and recite words with the letter x.
>   Use these words in sentences to build vocabulary.

**Materials:**
>   Book of verses: Ant to Zinnia Nature's ABC's
>   ABC activity sheet for the letter *x*
>   Paper and crayons
>   Two sheets of white paper per student
>   Scissors, glue, thread or yarn
>   White tissue paper
>   A picture of a human skeleton

**Procedure:**
>   Read the verse for the word *x-ray* and show the illustration.
>   Pass out paper, crayons, and the handout for the letter *x*.
>   Write the letter *x* and the word *x-ray*.
>   Draw the x-ray fish. Students do the same.
>   Write and recite, "*x* says *xx*" as in the words *extra*, *exam*, and *exit*.
>   Write and use each word in a sentence.
>   Students may copy and/or color the activity sheet for the letter *x*.

**Activities:**
>   We are similar to each other.
>   We all have skeletons that are made of bones.
>   Show students a picture of a human skeleton and the picture of the x-ray fish.

>   Let's make x-ray fish banners:
>   An adult shows you how to draw two x-ray fish the same size.
>   You can use the fish in the activity sheet as an example.
>   Use a black marker to draw bones on both fish and cut these out.
>   Glue the edges of the two fish together but leave an opening so that you can stuff the fish with tissue paper. Now glue the edges all the way around.
>   Tape thread or yarn to the nose end of your fish and hang it wherever you like.

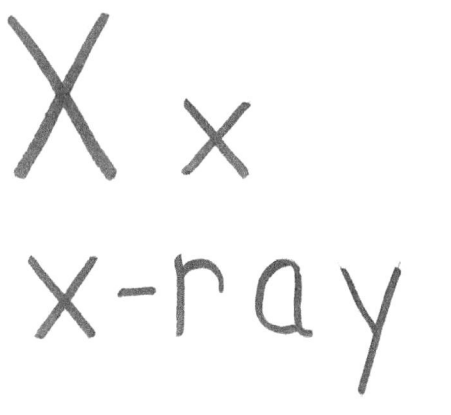

X x

x-ray

Lesson 25: **Yo-Yo**

**Objectives:**
Recognize the letter *y* and learn its sound.
Write the letter *y* and the word *yo-yo*.
Learn words that begin with the letter *y*.
Write sentences with words that begin with *y*.
Build vocabulary and improve comprehension.

**Materials:**
Book of verses: Ant to Zinnia Nature's ABC's
ABC activity sheet for the letter *y*
Paper and crayons
Percussion instruments: drum and/or rattles
Something to play lively tunes on

**Procedure:**
Read the verse for the word *yo-yo* and show the illustration.
Pass out paper, crayons, and the handout for the letter *y*.
Write the letter *y* and the word *yo-yo*.
Draw a yo-yo. Students do the same.
Write and recite, "*y* says *yuh*" as in the words *yarn*, *yam*, and *yak*.
Write and use each word in a sentence.

**Activities:**
What do toy yo-yo's have to do with nature?
They move up and down, back and forth and round and round.
Can you think of an animal in nature that can move like a yo-yo?
The humming bird can move in any direction just like a yo-yo on a string.

Let's dance:
Put on some lively music or play percussion instruments like a drum and rattles.
Move to the rhythm of the music.
Reach up to the sky.
Bend down and touch the ground.
Step to your left side and then step to your right side.
Gently swing your arms side to side and round in a circle going both directions.
Walk in a circle, first to your left then turn to your right.
Round and round like a yo-yo we go. Be careful not to get dizzy!

Y y
yo-yo

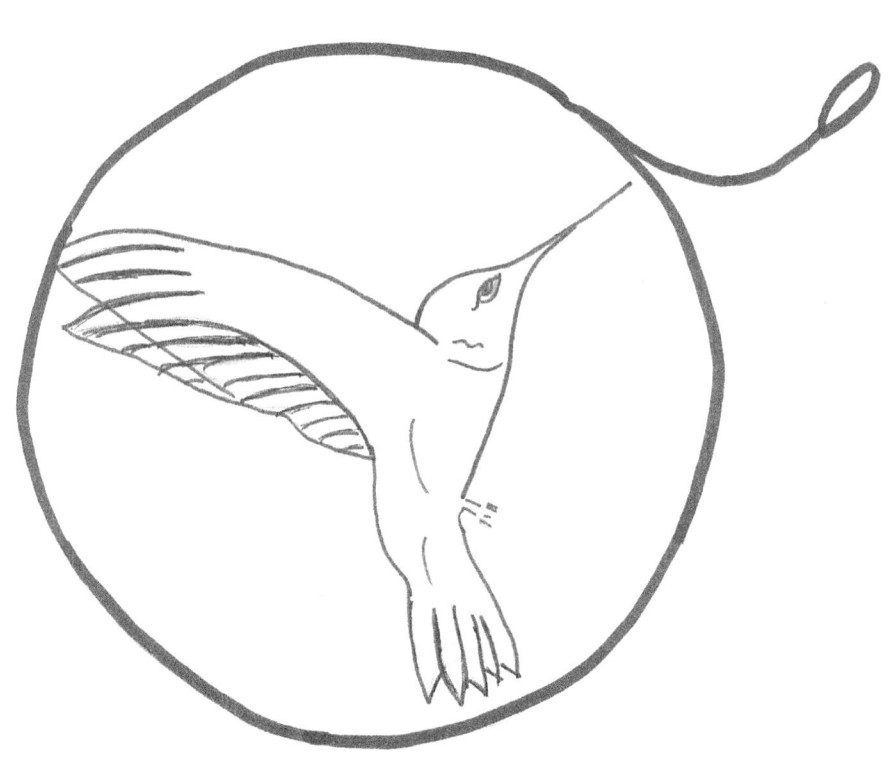

Lesson 26: **ZINNIA**

**Objectives:**
Recognize the letter *z* and learn its sound.
Write the letter *z* and the word *zinnia*.
Write and recite words that begin with the letter *z* in sentences.
Do one or all three activities below to inspire imagination.

**Materials:**
Book of verses: Ant to Zinnia Nature's ABC's
ABC activity sheet for the letter *z*
Paper and crayons
Smooth rock like a river rock
Inexpensive acrylic paint and brushes
Packet of wildflower seeds

**Procedure:**
Read the verse for the word zinnia and show the illustration.
Pass out paper, crayons and the activity sheet for the letter *z*.
Write the letter *z* and the word *zinnia*. Draw a *zinnia*. Students do the same.
Write and recite, *"z says zzz" as* in the words *zero, zebra and zipper*.
Write and use each word in a sentence.

**Activities:**
Let's color flowers:
Draw or trace zinnia flower like the one in the activity book.
Color your favorite flowers like: roses, tulips and irises and create a colorful garden.

Let's make a rock painting:
It is also fun to decorate a garden or home with rock paintings of zinnia and flowers.
Draw a zinnia or favorite flower on a smooth rock with a pencil or marker.
Use acrylic paint or markers to make colorful flowers on rocks.

Let's do a garden project:
Another fun project is to take a packet of wild flower seeds and spread them on the ground in your yard. Gently rake them into the ground and water them daily for about five days and then once a week. Enjoy your field of colorful wild flowers! This is a good project to do in the springtime.

# Z z

## zinnia

Hyda Maria Dougherty is a native New Mexican and a lifelong resident of Santa Fe. Through both the development of early-learning curriculum and direct instruction, she has been a reliable advocate of children's literacy through the course of her career.

Drawing inspiration from nature and from the stories, songs, and dances of the Indigenous cultures of the region. Ms. Dougherty has created this fun and engaging literacy-focused learning tool. With, *"Ant to Zinnia Nature's ABC's"* and its companion book, *"Ant to Zinnia Nature Activities"* in hand, children will be better equipped to begin—and share—their own imaginative adventures through literature and its respective arts.

The "Ant to Zinnia" set is a must-have for the beginning or challenged reader: a playful educational experience for the child; and a solid, trustworthy choice for grown-up curators of the young reader's library.

*Photo by Daniel Quat. Bio written by Rosemary Diaz.*